A BUG'S DAY

A Dragonfly's Day

by Elizabeth Neuenfeldt
Illustrated by Claudia Marianno

BLASTOFF! MISSIONS

BLASTOFF! MISSIONS, AN IMPRINT OF BELLWETHER MEDIA BY FLUTTERBEE

BLASTOFF! MISSIONS

Blastoff! Missions takes you on a learning adventure! Colorful illustrations and exciting narratives highlight cool facts about our world and beyond. Read the mission goals and follow the narrative to gain knowledge, build reading skills, and have fun!

Traditional Nonfiction

Narrative Nonfiction

Blastoff! Universe

MISSION GOALS

- FIND YOUR SIGHT WORDS IN THE BOOK.
- LEARN WHAT A DRAGONFLY DOES IN A DAY.
- LEARN HOW A DRAGONFLY CATCHES PREY.

This edition first published in 2027 by Bellwether Media, Inc.

For information regarding permission, write to Bellwether Media, Inc., Attention: Permissions Department, 3500 American Blvd W, Suite 150, Bloomington, MN 55431.

Library of Congress Cataloging-in-Publication Data

Names: Neuenfeldt, Elizabeth author | Marianno, Claudia, illustrator. Title: A dragonfly's day / by Elizabeth Neuenfeldt; illustrated by Claudia Marianno.
Description: Minneapolis, Minnesota : Bellwether Media, Inc, 2027. | Series: A bug's day | Includes bibliographical references and index. | Audience: Ages 5-8 | Audience: Grades 2-3 | Summary: "Vibrant illustrations accompany information about dragonflies. The narrative nonfiction text is intended for students in kindergarten through third grade."-- Provided by publisher.
Identifiers: LCCN 2026001594 (print) | LCCN 2026001595 (ebook) | ISBN 9798898800864 (library binding) | ISBN 9798898802103 (ebook)
Subjects: LCSH: Dragonflies--Juvenile literature | Insects--Juvenile literature
Classification: LCC QL520 .N48 2027 (print) | LCC QL520 (ebook)
LC record available at https://lccn.loc.gov/2026001594
LC ebook record available at https://lccn.loc.gov/2026001595

Editor: Betsy Rathburn Designer: Laura Sowers

Printed in the United States of America, North Mankato, MN.

This is **Blastoff Jimmy**! He is here to help you on your mission and share fun facts along the way!

Table of Contents

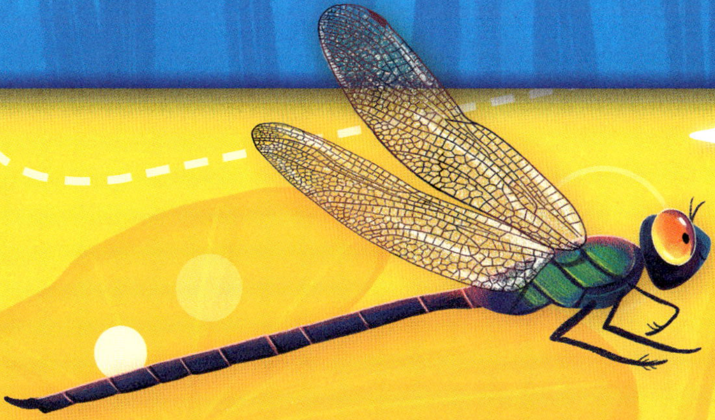

Good Morning!

JIMMY SAYS
There are around 7,000 kinds of dragonflies.

It is a beautiful morning. The dragonfly rests on a blade of grass.

Soon it will start its day!

wings

The sun rises over the trees.
The dragonfly's wings shine
in the sun.

It uses the sun to warm itself
up. Soon it will take flight!

Flying High

The dragonfly flies in the air.
It **glides** around a nearby pond.

It uses its big eyes to look for **prey**.
It hunts moths and mosquitoes.

eye

The dragonfly darts in many directions as it flies over the water.

Was that a mosquito?
The dragonfly flies backwards
to get closer.

JIMMY SAYS

Some dragonflies can fly over 30 miles (48 kilometers) per hour!

The dragonfly sees it is a mosquito. It will be a tasty treat!

The dragonfly forms its legs into a basket. It catches the food!

Look out! There is a spider web ahead. It could trap the dragonfly.

The dragonfly quickly zips around it.

predator

Suddenly, a bird flies by. This **predator** tries to eat the dragonfly.

But the dragonfly is fast. It quickly gets away. Phew! That was close!

Laying Eggs

Look! The dragonfly found a **mate**. They fly together.

The female dragonfly lays eggs in the water. Both dragonflies fly off!

Soon the eggs will break open. Those **nymphs** will grow into dragonflies.

Dragonflies have busy lives!

All About Dragonflies

Body Parts

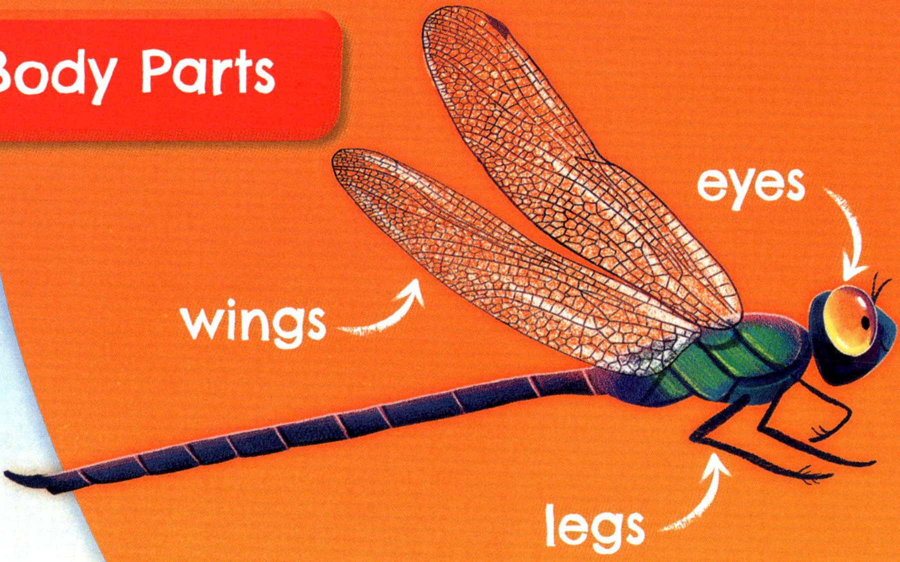

Things Seen

pond

mosquito

bird

Glossary

glides–moves smoothly

mate–a partner

nymphs–young dragonflies

predator–an animal that hunts other animals for food

prey–animals that are hunted by other animals for food

To Learn More

AT THE LIBRARY

Gieseke, Tyler. *Turning Into a Dragonfly.* Minneapolis, Minn.: Pop!, 2022.

Kenney, Karen Latchana. *All About Dragonflies.* Minneapolis, Minn.: Jump!, 2024.

Ruby, Rex. *A Dragonfly Grows.* Bloomington, Minn.: Bearport Publishing Company, 2026.

ON THE WEB

FACTSURFER

Factsurfer.com gives you a safe, fun way to find more information.

1. Go to www.factsurfer.com.

2. Enter "a dragonfly's day" into the search box and click 🔍.

3. Select your book cover to see a list of related content.

BEYOND THE MISSION

> WHAT FACT FROM THE BOOK DID YOU THINK WAS THE MOST INTERESTING?

> DRAW A DRAGONFLY. WHICH BODY PARTS DO YOU THINK ARE MOST IMPORTANT?

> WHAT ARE SOME ACTIVITIES THAT YOU DO EVERY DAY?

Index